ROAR!

ROAR!
Copyright © 2019 by Cinda S. Lonsway

Published by new72media
d/b/a new72publishing
www.new72media.com

Printed in the United States of America

ISBN: 978-1-946054-11-1 (Hardback)
ISBN: 978-1-946054-10-4 (eBook)

All rights reserved. This book or any portion thereof may not be reproduced or used in any manner whatsoever without the express written permission of the publisher except for the use of brief quotations in a book review.

ROAR!

CINDA STEVENS LONSWAY
Illustrated by Manon Doyle

DEDICATIONS

CINDA

ROAR! is dedicated to Mother Earth, the giver and creator of all life. May we protect Her always.

And to the youth—our future is in your hands. Join in harmony to shift Mother Earth on Her axis and create positive change.

MANON

The paintings in ROAR! are dedicated to all who are finding their voice in this world.

ROAR!

It began as a whisper...

ROAR!

...one woman
leaning into the ear
of another.

"Do you feel it?"
she asked.

Then...
She whispered to another,
"Do you feel it?"

And it began to spread,
...this whisper...
from one woman
to another,
to another,
whispering,
"Do you feel it?"
"Do you feel it?"

do you feel it?

ROAR!

The question was asked once,
then twice...
then grew to
ten hundred whispers
around the world.

Women wondering
what it was
they were feeling.

The whispering pulsed
as need for the answer grew.

"Do you feel it?"

ROAR!

The rhythm became
stronger, bolder,
as it spread to their hearts.

Knowing not
what was the whisper
or what was the heartbeat,
for the two became one.

More and more women
began to feel the pounding
of a need not yet understood
and the rumbling began to stir
the earth under their feet.

ROAR!

One woman stood.
She planted her feet firmly into the soil,
raised her voice from a whisper
and shouted,
"Enough!"

The woman next to her stood.
With her fists pumping the sky,
she yelled,
"Enough!"

"Enough! Enough!"
shouted another, another, and another.
Women, each holding firm in their stance,
arms above their heads,
"Enough!"
"Enough!"
"Enough!"

enough. free me.

ROAR!

But it wasn't **enough**
to stop the growing whisper.

It is never **enough**
when you are a woman...
for women aren't always heard.

We are taken for granted,
too much is expected,
too much is asked.

ROAR!

We give.
We cry.
We shout.

But it is never **enough**
to be noticed,
appreciated,
worshiped.

ROAR!

The whispering,
the rhythm,
continued....

It did not slow down.

The pounding expanded,
and the hearts of the women
grew more restless.

ROAR!

Their whispering
was the beginning....

Their individual shouts
were not **enough**.

ROAR!

Then one woman
clasped the hand of her sister,
who clasped the hand of her mother,
who clasped the hand of her friend.

One solid clasp
from another, to another.

Now a sound of women
bonding themselves together,
united with the rhythm
already sounding in their souls.

ROAR!

Hand-to-hand.
Heart-to-heart.

Then something new happened....

In the comfort of unity,
in the safety of numbers,
another moment
for another sound.

It came not from one,
but from the consciousness
of all women.

ROAR!

The sound came from
the women
of the Now.
Mothers, grandmothers,
sisters, daughters.

It came from
the women
of the Ancients.

ROAR!

And it came from
the ultimate mother,
Mother Earth.

For the sound resonated
with each and every woman,
who had planted her feet
into the soil to yell,
"Enough!"

ROAR!

Then...
the women realized...

...the rhythm they felt
was not to be stopped...

...the rhythm
was their calling...

...waking them up
to their time.

ROAR!

Their time...
to yell, "Enough!"
but not to stop
the rhythm
of their newly
awakened hearts.

Their time...
to yell, "Enough!"
to stop
the atrocities done
to their mothers,
grandmothers,
sisters, daughters,
their ancestors
and their planet.

ROAR!

This understanding...
...this awakening...
...began to make
their feet stomp
and in unison
their voices raised.

What was once a whisper
became a rumble.

The rumble
turned into a
gentle roar.

ROAR!

But...
a roar
is not meant
to be gentle.

A roar
is meant to be
fierce and powerful!

The roar
grew in tones
of bass and treble,
lows and highs,
in young and old throats.

ROAR!

A sound...
not heard in centuries....

A sound...
of battle cries
led by priestesses and queens....

A sound...
that could no longer
be contained,
or ignored.

They roared,
"NO MORE!"
"NO MORE!"
"NO MORE!"

ROAR!

Then...
one-by-one,
by tens, by thousands,
they roared their loyalty
to each other,
to their families,
to their sisters,
to their brothers,
and
Mother Earth.

ROAR!

"NO MORE!"
the women roared,
"will I see myself
as unworthy,
as unattractive,
as less than more!"

ROAR!

"NO MORE!"
they roared,
"will I walk by hungry children
and not feed them!"

"NO MORE!"
said the Roar,
"will I ignore a bruised
and battered woman
and not invite her
into my home."

ROAR!

"NO MORE!"

"NO MORE!"
they roared,
"will we know of
girls and women
being sold,
or violated,
or silenced,
and do nothing!"

"NO MORE!
will we send our boys
off to fight wars!"

ROAR!

"NO MORE!
will we tolerate
toxic waste being thrown out
where only the poor can live."

"NO MORE!
will we stand by and let
the oceans, mountains, air,
forests, and fields
be ruined of their natural beauty,
or polluted with poison!"

ROAR!

The ROAR grew,
and the women grew stronger.

Those who couldn't hear it before...
stirred.
They became nervous, scared...
altered.
What did this mean?

These powerful women roaring,
demanding, pledging
to change the world...
...it couldn't be good, this roaring...
right?

WRONG!

ROAR!

For now...
nothing could stop the
ROAR! of
"NO MORE!"
The women swayed.
The women stomped.
The women continued to ROAR!

Men, good men,
stepped into the circles
and they began to roar.

The youth,
who once thought there was no hope for their future,
took to the circle. They clasped hands
with their parents, their teachers, their friends,
and in the innocence of a new adventure,
joined in the harmony of millions.

ROAR!

The
ROAR! of
"NO MORE!"
now one solid vibration,
surrounded the world,
and the earth began to
rumble under their feet.

Mother Earth
began to shake.
To quake.
She shuddered, and sputtered,
she stretched, and she pulled,
she groaned, and moaned
...and then it happened....

ROAR!

Never before
in the history of recorded events
has the world ever
shifted on it axis.

In one bit of a final
shoulder shake,
Atlas turned Mother Earth
to the light...
...to the light of nurture, of nature,
to the light of bravery, of truth,
to the light of change, of hope,
to the light of Love and of Spirit.

ROAR!

Earth was turned
to the
LIGHT of WOMEN,
to a brighter moon in the sky
shining down
among the masses
of committed souls
around the world.

ROAR!

Then all fell silent.

Parents brought their children home
from the streets and from war.

Books were delivered to schools
and girls entered their doors.

Fists and threats were no longer raised,
and meals were shared with families.

Waste dumps were cleaned up,
trees were planted,
and oceans cleansed.

ROAR!

The power of
the feminine full moon shined
equal to the masculine sun.

And just like that,
peace was formed.
Balance restored.

For when there is peace,
there is room for
the Divine,
and when the Divine
is with women,
there is nothing they can't do...
like rock the world on its axis
or
feel a whisper coming on.

ROAR!

"Do you feel it?"

If you do...and I know you do...
if you are woman alive today...
you do.

I ask you to feel it.
Unite with it.
Create a stirring.
Spread this whisper.

Begin your own
ROAR! of
"NO MORE!"

ROAR!

Join me, please...

I whisper to you now....

THE STORY OF ROAR!

In May of 2010, my entire life changed. The change came about in the most unexpected way—via my social media feed, from a news video someone shared with me. This video grabbed my attention and I couldn't look away—footage which gripped at my care and concern for the environment. The video streamed footage of an oil leak in the Gulf of Mexico. I watched in horror as hundreds of thousands of gallons of oil spewed from the bottom of the ocean. I watched in agony as sea life and animals were drenched in life-threatening poison. I watched in disgust as politicians and petroleum corporations refused to take ownership.

I watched in overwhelming *sadness*—as *no one* did *anything* to stop it!

I was sickened—*sickened.*

As each plume of black goo mixed with the water, I felt my heart break and my spirit collapse. Something was terribly wrong, horribly not okay, dreadfully threatening...to not just the sea life, but to all of life. THIS wasn't oil...THIS was blood...THIS was Mother Earth hemorrhaging.... And if we didn't stop this quickly...she could die.

The leaders—*our* leaders, the government—*our* government, and the oil tycoons' lack of concern or regard or attempt to save HER fueled a sense of urgency, a sense of activism in me that I'd never felt before.

I screamed at my computer screen, *"If SHE dies, we all die. Don't you bastards see that?"*

HER suffering apparently didn't matter. SHE didn't matter. I saw a parallel...a parallel in how Mother Earth and women have been treated with disgrace, disrespect, and disregard for eons. I sympathized, I empathized, I identified with Mother Earth.

Years ago, in 1981, I was a victim of a violent crime. After it happened, I ran away from the neighborhood, the criminal and the memory of the crime. For years, I denied that my perpetrator's actions had harmed me. I pretended that nothing had happened. Denial didn't serve my recovery. Finally, I found my healing and with that I found a calling to help others.[1] I couldn't and wouldn't allow denial or pretending that nothing was wrong, again. I refuse to watch as another is victimized—man, woman or child—especially if it's our ultimate Mother.

When any woman, any mother suffers, we all do.

But what could I do? I couldn't spend either money or time to fly down to Florida and help clean up the mess. I didn't know how to stop the leak. I could write to my state senators, representatives, and members of the U.S. Congress, but that didn't feel like enough.

When any woman, any mother suffers, we all do.

Every night when I went to bed, I hoped for inspiration. Every night I chanted the words, I felt the words, I fell asleep to the words branded in my thoughts. Every night I wanted to scream out so the world could hear them too: "WHEN ANY WOMAN SUFFERS, ANY MOTHER SUFFERS, WE ALL DO!"

Some nights these words kept me awake. They began to create a life of their own...a rhythm...a pounding...that repeated itself, over and over.

"When any woman...*pound, pound*...any mother...*pound, pound*...suffers...*pound*...we all do."

The drumming was soft, but strong.

One night, along with the drumming, I began to hear whispering. The whispering grew louder and louder.

"Do you feel it? Do you feel it?"

The single whisper combined with other voices...women's voices. I heard them. I felt them. They were coming to life. They were giving me a message. They were demanding...demanding that their message be given a voice. The message grew and expanded until it was too big, too much for me to keep inside. I sprang out of bed, rushed downstairs and with determination to keep up, I wrote.

---

[1] *In 2017 I wrote a book about the attack, my healing and the awakening that came because of it*: I Know Now: A Woman's Healing: Violence to Victory, Trauma to Truth.

A few minutes later, I set the pen aside, picked up the paper and read. I read words that I didn't remember writing. I read words that were so powerful they made me weep. I read the words of a thousand plus women coming together, roaring to save each other, their families and their planet. I read the message given to me from Mother Earth.

I titled it *ROAR!*

The words have strength and power and a rhythm that is like nothing I've ever read. This short story is a parable, a poem, a declaration, a reclamation, a lesson for all of us. With their feet planted—grounded—in the earth, the women declare, "NO MORE!" and "ENOUGH!"

By the end of the story, the world—Earth and humanity—shifts on its axis and turns toward the light and power of women. The lesson, the message is clear: *Because of the action of women, the world is changed for the better.* Then all becomes quiet, peace is restored, and all is well.

I shared *ROAR!* with an inspirational author who is a friend of mine, Jack Armstrong. Jack told me through his tears that I needed to share it, and to share it now. Without another thought, I posted it as a "note" on Facebook and within hours it was shared across the globe...after a few days, it went viral. People from around the world asked if they could make *ROAR!* part of their rituals, part of their discussion groups, post it in their personal and professional blogs, and turn it into a stage production. It was translated into different languages.

I was asked to create a workshop around the essence of *ROAR!* and the energy of "NO MORE!" and "ENOUGH!" I was invited to travel across the northwest United States as a professional facilitator and speaker. I was queried about hosting my own internet TV show titled "ROAR!"

Many women wrote to me and shared that they were inspired to "ROAR!" and take action by giving a voice to their truth. Some stood up to their perpetrator. Others protested environmental wrongs. Many became advocates for those who couldn't do it for themselves. Their stories were powerful...their bravery, mighty...their commitment to their truth, life altering. The letters came, and I watched the world change around me.

ROAR!

I had used my pen and my keyboard as my tools for activism, and it appeared to make a difference. My words became a powerful yet peaceful way to create positive change. Whether it made a difference in getting the oil leak plugged, the beaches cleaned, the animals treated and released, I don't know. But I do know this: the rhythm that I felt that night, the voices I heard, the message that I wrote and then shared...resonated and still resonates with others across the globe.

Today, the need for women to unite and "ROAR!" is greater than ever. It is time for them, for us, to no longer sit in silence, in the shadows, invisible. It is time for women, and the men who love them, to act when they see wrong... to not stop the "ROAR!" until it is right.

It is time.

Women. Stand up and give voice to your truth.

Women. Your truth is powerful.

Women. Your voice is necessary for positive change.

ROAR!

"ENOUGH!"

"NO MORE!"

It is time.

Do you feel it?

ILLUSTRATIONS

	"Whisper," 2013 10"x13" acrylic on canvas	page 7
	"Lean In," 2013 10.5"x13" acrylic on canvas	page 9
	"Do You Feel It?" 2013 8"x11" acrylic on canvas	page 11
	"Wonder," 2013 8"x11.25" acrylic on canvas	page 13
	"Her Rhythm," 2013 9"x12" acrylic on watercolor paper	page 15
	"Enough!" 2013 8"x11" acrylic on canvas	page 17
	"Silenced," 2013 9"x12" acrylic on watercolor paper	page 19
	"We Cry," 2013 9"x12" acrylic on canvas	page 21

ROAR!

	"Restless Heart," 2011 18"x24" textured acrylic on gessobord	page 23
	"Innocent Fierceness," 2013 9.5"x12.25" acrylic on canvas	page 25
	"Bonded," 2011 6"x9" acrylic on watercolor paper	page 27
	"I Will," 2011 6"x9" acrylic on watercolor paper	page 29
	"Women of Ages," 2013 24"x18" acrylic collage (with words of ROAR! glued underneath) on gessoboard 2.25" panel	pages 30-31
	"Within," 2013 8"x10" acrylic on claybord	page 35
	"Women of My Soul," 2011 18"x24" acrylic and collage on stretched canvas	page 37
	"My Voice," 2011 9"x12.25" acrylic on watercolor paper	page 39
	"Warrior," 2013 8.25"x11" acrylic on canvas	page 41

	"Queen of No More!" 2013 10"x13.25" acrylic on canvas	page 43
	"Courageous," 2011 12"x16" acrylic on gessobord 1.5" panel	page 45
	"Worthy," 2013 10.25"x13" acrylic on canvas	page 47
	"You've Got This," 2011 10"x13" acrylic on canvas	page 49
	"Be the Change," 2013 10"x13" acrylic on canvas	page 51
	"Protect Her," 2013 9"x12.25" acrylic on watercolor paper	page 53
	"She Guides Me," 2011 8.25"x11.25" acrylic on canvas	page 55
	"Love Surrounds Me," 2013 8"x11" acrylic on canvas	page 57
	"Possibilities," 2013 8"x11.25" acrylic on canvas	page 59

ROAR!

	"Shift the World," 2010 5"x7" acrylic on paper inside private journal	page 61
	"To the Light of Women," 2013 10.25"x13" acrylic on canvas	page 63
	"I AM," 2013 9"x12" acrylic on watercolor paper	page 65
	"With the Divine," 2013 9.75"x13.25" acrylic on canvas	page 67
	"Hope," 2010 8"x10.75" acrylic on canvas	page 69
	"It's Time," 2013 10.25"x13" acrylic on canvas	page 71

ACKNOWLEDGEMENTS

CINDA

ROAR! is a gift, a powerful gift that came through me to give to the world. Whatever energy it is…Gaia, Archangel Ariel, my own heart and knowing… I want to thank that voice, that presence, that entity for choosing me.

Thank you to my husband, Scott, and my sons, Eric and Ryan, for giving me the space to experiment with my newfound and public form of activism and feminism. Thank you to my beloved friends for believing in me and in this message. Thank you to my Facebook community, back in 2010, for sharing *ROAR!* by sending it around the world and utilizing it in ways I could have never imagined. Thank you to the many of you who participated in my *ROAR!* workshops—leading the cries of "NO MORE!" and "ENOUGH!"

Thank you to Manon Doyle for jumping at the chance to paint my words. Your art moves my soul every time I see it. Thank you to new72publishing's leader Kelli Lair, and to my devoted editor, Mary L. Holden, for your continued belief in my words.

MANON

Thank you to my partner, Rob. We started dating at the very beginning of this project and his continuous support has meant the world to me.

Thank you to my mom Carmen, my daughter Alex, my best friend Nathalie, my good friend Laura and my dearest friend Cathy. These women have shown me how strong we can be as women. I have learned so much from each of you.

Thank you to Cinda Stevens Lonsway for inviting me to be part of this amazing project and for trusting me with her words.

Author Cinda Stevens Lonsway

Cinda Stevens Lonsway has passion for writing, storytelling, and speaking about the truths she's discovered as a woman. Being a daughter, friend, student, employee, volunteer, traveler, hostess, wife, and mother, Cinda writes of these experiences to empower readers. She also works as a spiritual counselor, workshop facilitator, and speaker.

In 2017, Cinda published her memoir, *I Know Now...A Woman's Healing: Violence to Victory, Trauma to Truth*. Having fought off an attacker at the age of 19, she writes of her experience suppressing the trauma, suffering the memories when they'd resurface, and finally breaking down to the point of discovering a process of healing that is still going on every day. The importance of her memoir is significant at this time in history, when women are finding a new ability to stand up for themselves and speak their truths.

Cinda lives in Portland, Oregon with her husband, two adult sons, a Golden Retriever, and a high-maintenance cat. She writes nonfiction, novels, and stories for children.

Visit her website: www.CindaStevensLonsway.com

Artist Manon Doyle

Manon Doyle is an all-around creative. Her passions include being a silversmith, jeweler, and painter. She is the cofounder and creator of Sisters of the Sun, so named because she feels a true kinship with women. The sun represents light, energy, life and spirituality. The heart inside the sun is her logo. It represents warmth, love, compassion, and the spirit of giving.

Currently, Manon works with sterling silver, inserting gemstones into the metal to create one-of-a-kind pieces of jewelry. She stamps inspiring messages on the back of her silver creations. She welcomes the opportunity to work closely with clients in creating custom orders.

She lives in Scottsdale, Arizona

Visit her Etsy page: www.sistersofthesun.etsy.com

Follow her blog: www.sistersofthesun.com

The Story of Cinda and Manon

In 2011, almost a year after "ROAR!" went viral on the Internet, Cinda came across a piece of art on a friend's Facebook page. The painting was of a field of hearts swaying in the wind with the saying, "Can you feel it?" The comparison to the "Do you feel it?" from "ROAR!" caused Cinda's heart to skip a beat.

With some research, Cinda found Manon's website and could see that her paintings were in alignment with the energy of "ROAR!" After Cinda connected with Manon, she learned that Manon had been painting women as a way to find her own strength, power and voice. When Manon read "ROAR!" she was altered, felt deeply connected to the words, and was honored to be asked by Cinda to paint her inspiration. Little did she know that the process would became part of her own healing journey.

The collaboration between these two women—who unknowingly tapped into the same energy, around the same time, using their own artistic media to express what they were feeling—is captured in this vision board that Manon created. They celebrate their journey together by inviting you to join with them in your own *ROAR!* of "NO MORE!" and "ENOUGH!"

Do you feel it?

ROAR!